The World's Shortest Wine Book*

maybe...

The World's Shortest Wine Book*

*maybe...

21 ways to get more out of a bottle of wine

SIMON WOODS

The World's Shortest Wine Book:
21 ways to get more out of a bottle of wine.

By Simon Woods

First published in 2014 by Simon Woods, 37 Wool Road, Dobcross, Oldham OL3 5NS, United Kingdom

ISBN-13: 978-0993000607

ISBN-10: 0993000606

DEDICATION

To two magnificent grandpas:
My Dad – for his picky palate and sense of fun
Howard – for being generous at all times

Introduction

First of all, if you haven't already got one, go and pour yourself a glass of wine, I'll still be here when you get back...

All set now? Good. My name's Simon Woods, and I've been writing about, talking about, enthusing about wine for 25 years. I've written a number of books in that time too, and although some of them have won major awards, none has been as short as this one.

There are more than 100 wine books on the shelves in front of my desk, but rather too many of them fall into the 'worthy' category. They're like textbooks, packed with info, but a bit on the heavy side - and certainly too heavy to read in bed...

Which is where 'The World's Shortest Wine Book' comes in. The main reason I've written the book is because I've met so many people who just don't know where to begin an exploration of the wonderful world of wine. Those textbooks are all very well, but you've got to start with something a little more user-friendly.

Also, a small part of my goal in each of these 21 short chapters is to bring at least a suggestion of a smile to your face. If it were in print form, I'd suggest keeping a copy next to the toilet – a chapter per visit, maybe two if you've eaten something dodgy...

The book's also a bit different from others in that I'm not going to give you any shopping lists of what to go out and buy. In the first Kindle version of this book, at the end of each chapter I gave a little spiel about a wine that had inspired that particular section. Bit of a change this time round. You'll find 21 different types of wines, not from different regions, nor particular grape varieties but...well, read a couple and hopefully you'll get the picture. And at the end of the book, I'd love to hear from you whether you've had any wines that fell into some of these brackets.

So grab a glass and – oh, you've got one already. Well let's get going...

Before we get to Chapter 1, tell me, which of these sounds better?

'21 ideas to get more out of a bottle of wine'
OR
'24 ideas to get more out of a bottle of wine'

I'm not quite sure why, but I plumped for the first.
However, I DID actually write 24 chapters.

If you want to read the extra 3,
go to simonwoods.com/shortest-chapters
and I'll send them to you.

Now read on…

Get some decent glasses

The easiest way to get more out of a bottle of wine? Buy some decent glasses. When it comes to things like kitchen knives, hand tools and shoes, you've probably learned through hard experience that it's not worth resorting to the bargain basement. It's the same with wine glasses. Over the course of a glass's lifetime, you'll pour several hundred £s, $s, €s worth of grog into it, so it's a sensible investment. And the good news is that while you can fork out serious money for stemware (hate that word), you don't have to.

So how can you spot a decent glass? A couple of pointers. Firstly, it needs to be shaped like a horseshoe, or a capital letter 'U' with the top bits squeezed together. And secondly, when you pour in a normal measure of wine – let's say a sixth of a regular bottle – it shouldn't be more than a third full.

Why? So that when you give the glass a good swirl to release the aromas, the wine has plenty of room to swish around, while the tapering shape of the glass funnels those (hopefully) nice smells towards your hooter.

Have patterns and cut glass if you like, but I prefer a plain, unadorned format – a nice wine swirling around the inside is all the visuals you need. If you need a starting point, IKEA's Hederlig range cost £1.40/US$1.99 each, and they're perfectly adequate for all but the most picky drinkers.

The wine that breaks the ice

Despite what I've said above, I'm not going to send the wine police round if I hear about you serving wine in chipped Paris goblets. In fact one of the most memorable wines I ever had was drunk out of plastic picnic cups on the beach at Margaret River in Western Australia.

I was in my mid-twenties and had just met my Perth-based cousin Bill for the first time in over 15 years. Conversation was aided by a bottle of 1982 Yarra Yering Dry Red No 1, one of the greatest Cabernets in Australia. Yes, it would probably have been better out of a proper glass, but the wine still tasted great, and was a brilliant catalyst for the start of a great relationship (not to mention a rather boisterous evening...)

Getting sniffy

While we're on the subject of sniffing and swirling, I might as well explain what the point is. It's to do with first impressions. Think of parties. Ever met those folk who seem initially fascinating, but after five minutes, you're making excuses and heading off to the other side of the room? Conversely, ever come across those people who seem a little shy to start with, but then go on to reveal that they've climbed Everest/have a pet panther/speak 10 languages? Some wines bound out of the glass to greet you, but then fall flat. Others take a while to come out of their shell, but the wait – the swirling – is worth it.

As for the sniffing, most of our flavour perception is to do with our nose – have you noticed how your sense of taste disappears when you have a cold? Or how holding your nose when you have food you don't like diminishes the taste? And gets you funny looks in restaurants?

Our tongues only detect taste sensations: sweet, salty, sour and bitter are the classic four, umami (savouriness) is now recognised as a fifth, while some people would also throw piquancy, metallicity, fattiness, dryness (as in tannins in wine) and coolness (as in mint) into the mix. It's actually our noses that pick up the precise flavours – sniffing the wine simply means that we get more bang for our buck from it.

And once you've put the wine in your mouth, don't chug it down straight away. When we chew our food slowly or swish a wine around our mouths, more aromas are released, and these can make their way again to our noses via what is called the retronasal passage. You might look a bit like a ruminating hamster, so don't overdo it on first dates, but it does mean that you're getting more and more flavour out of that precious wine.

The worst wine ever

Some wines smell great, others just smell. It's a two-way contest for the worst wine I've ever sniffed and – foolishly – let pass my lips. One was Cru des Ptolomies from Egypt, allegedly a white wine, although brown would be more accurate. Think bad home-made 'sherry' with notes of sweat and maybe a touch of turps.

The other was one I made from a kit for a magazine piece. I suspected that producing half-decent Chardonnay and Cabernet Sauvignon in 'just 7 days!' was not on the cards, and I was right. The white was better than the red, but only in the sense that Boyzone were better than Westlife. The red however... Words fail me, so I'll just pass on the reaction from an unfortunate friend who bravely tried it with me: "It's the sort of wine that made me wish I was driving."

Don't underspend

Of course, no glass is going to help you get much out of a wine that's not very precious in the first place. This should come as no surprise. Can you buy a classy car from a scuzzy back street dealer? Are the latest fashions available at next door's garage sale? Do you expect great food at the local Greasy Joe's? No, no, no. Or at least the majority of the time, no. Most of us realise that in such matters, it's worth going somewhere special and paying a little bit more to find something decent.

Yet for some reason wine isn't viewed in the same way. Maybe it all boils down to why people drink in the first place. If it's purely to get drunk, then by all means buy whatever does the biz for the lowest price per unit of intoxication.

But surely there's more to wine than just getting off your face? It's not vodka that 'gladdens the heart of man' in The Bible. It wasn't lager that Robert Louis Stevenson referred to as 'bottled poetry'. And when Louis Pasteur wrote of the 'healthiest and most health-giving of drinks', he didn't have Bacardi Breezer in mind. If your life is such that you need to get blotto to enjoy it more, you don't need a wine book, you need therapy.

So then we get onto the enjoyability of wine. There's not much out-and-out bad wine made these days, but there's an ocean of bland wine, the grapey equivalent of lift music. Your taste buds deserve more than that, so treat them at least once a month. Spend more. Not much more, but a few dollars/pounds more.

Then for special occasions, push the boat out and spend double what you'd normally do – and for the record, a new series of *The Bridge* is a special occasion...

The cheap wine that overdelivers
Inexpensive wine can still have personality, if you know where to look. An especially happy hunting ground is South West France, with the best bargains being the whites of Côtes de Gascogne and Saint Mont – if you need a producer name, look for Plaimont Producteurs.

Most special offers are not very special

But just because it's a special occasion doesn't mean that you should resort to 'special' offers. Which brings me on to an old chestnut that goes something like this:-

Q: How do you make a small fortune in the wine industry?
A: Start with a large one...

Oh, how we in the trade laugh when that's trotted out for the umpteenth time. But behind the cheesy line, there's a truth to be learned. If you want to make pots of cash, sell bottled water, wedding cakes, popcorn, mattresses, designer jeans and numerous other items – just don't expect to strike it big with wine.

An honest local wine merchant will seldom add more than 40% to what they pay for a bottle – that's got to cover rent, rates, utility bills and staff wages, leaving very little in the way of profit. If they were to mark that bottle down to half-price, they'd be making a 30% loss.

So how come some companies are able to do half-price sales and other special offers? Well, let's be kind to start with and say that perhaps they have surplus stock they need to shift in order to make space for new arrivals. It does happen, and if you move quickly in some of the January bin-end sales, you can pick up a bargain.

But I'm not talking about someone offering their last 23 bottles of something at a keen price, I'm thinking of those places – supermarkets usually – where 'half-price' has become people's favourite brand. Watch out in many stores every November. Lurking somewhere in store will be a ropey Champagne no-one's ever heard of at a vastly inflated price. Then two weeks before Christmas, Shazaam! ***HALF-PRICE CHAMPAGNE WHILE STOCKS LAST***

The truth with this and virtually all the other half-price offers is that the reduction simply brings the wines back down to what they were worth in the first place. Anyone who pays the full price is a mug, and anyone who thinks they're getting a bargain is deluded.

The bargain buy wine
Looking back on my best wine bargain ever, I was probably acting as a fence. Was stocking shelves in a wine shop one day when someone came in offering some nobby Champagnes – Krug and Dom Pérignon to be precise – for a very sharp price. Mathematical brain whirring, I quickly worked out that if I bought a dozen bottles, I could sell eight to the shop and get the remaining four for free. So I did. Please forgive me, it was a long time ago...

Five + One

Not that I've a problem with you buying wine at the supermarket. Many of us stock up there, and we've probably all learned by now that if you buy in units of 6 or 12 bottles, you'll get a bit of a discount.

As for which 6/12 bottles, I'm happy for you to stock up on tried and trusted favourites, but I would encourage you to – in wine terms – get out a little more. In other words, put five old friends into that six-pack, but save the sixth space for experimentation.

It could be from a country you didn't know made wine. It could be a grape variety you've never heard of. But whatever it is, grab a bottle of something you've never heard of and give it a go.

It may be foul. Never mind, you'll know for next time, and you still have the other five to fall back on (and you can always take the offending bottle to a party). But it may be delicious – who knows, next time, it might even be the wine that makes up the first five bottles in that six-pack.

The wine that makes you revise your opinions

English fizz is quite rightly getting lots of plaudits at the moment – if you've not sampled it, it's a prime candidate for a sixth bottle in that wine carrier. However 20 years ago, the UK wine industry seemed mostly content to churn out rather fey wines made from peculiar Germanic grape varieties.

But there were already signs in the early 1990s that sparkling wine could be the future for UK producers. Nyetimber was the producer that first caught the public's eye with its fizz, but before it had released its first wines, I'd already sampled fizz from vineyards such as Wellow, Throwley and Thames Valley (a Gamay, made as a white wine) that made me think, "Watch this space."

There will always be another wine

If you do find that that 6th bottle has suddenly become flavour of the month, that's great. But don't go overboard. When you start really getting into wine, there'll come a day when you find something that is just so, so good that you're tempted to sell the dog and stock up on several cases instead. Now I don't want to dampen your enthusiasm, I love seeing people get excited about wine and wanting to share their passion, but if you can, dear reader, resist.

There are a number of reasons. Wines change with time, and not always for the better, and your tastes change too. Ever watched a rerun of a comedy you used to think was hilarious and wondered what you ever saw in it? Ever looked at a pic of yourself from 15 years ago and thought, "How could I ever have worn that?"?

But for me the best reason is variety.

Patient: Doctor, doctor, my family thinks I'm mad!
Doctor: Why's that?
Patient: Because I like sausages
Doctor: Well there's nothing wrong with that. Lots of people like sausages, I like sausages...
Patient: Oh really? You must come and see my collection sometime, I've got HUNDREDS!!

Stock up on just one wine – or even on one producer, or one vintage, or one region – and you miss out on all the squillions of other lovely wines out there. Six bottles, maybe; six cases, no. Yes, it may be lovely, and your local wine shop may have an unbeatable, never-to-be-repeated offer on it, but just remind yourself that there will always be another wine. Otherwise there is a real danger of you turning into Sausage Man...

The first really great wine you try

I'd have needed mortgage-level money to buy six cases of the first great wine I ever tried. I'd cycled across Melbourne to the premises of Paul de Burgh-Day, at the time one of Australia's premier French wine importers, for a tasting of 1985 Bordeaux.

Pick of a great bunch – and a wine whose mixture of intensity and finesse I can still recall – was Château Pétrus. The price tag was daunting, but I was all ready to slap AUS$250 on the counter and pedal home with a solitary bottle in my back pack. Until...'Sorry mate, it's all sold.' But as I said, there will always be another wine.

Not everyone likes the same wines

Another thing you'll soon discover if you start rabbiting on about the qualities of such-and-such a wine is that not everyone will agree with you. And we shouldn't be surprised about this, People can be into music and not like the same bands, genres, whatever. They can be into sport but not like athletics or F1 (yawnsville). They can be into travelling but hate sailing. So it is with wine. Some people like bold, hearty wines that leap out of the glass and strangle you. Others prefer wispy wines that take time to come out of their shell.

The truth is we all have different tastes. Serve a round of gin and tonics and then afterwards look at the empty glasses – half the lemons will have been chewed down to the rind, others will be untouched. My granny always put nutmeg in her apple pie: for me, it wrecked it, but she loved it. In the 1990s, a UK magazine put the same set of wines in front of two panels of tasters, one in London, the other in New York. The comments from both panels were similar, but while 'Big bold, oaky Chardonnay' was a positive in New York, it was a negative in London.

What's more, those tastes can change with time. Who has the same taste in music, clothes or boys/girls that they had when they were ten, or even twenty? Remember your first taste of beer? Or how much you used to like Coco Pops? Or how your favourite coffee was once milky with two sugars, whereas now it's an espresso?

Which explains why a typical wine shop has hundreds of different wines rather than just half a dozen.

The expensive wine that underdelivers
It happens to everyone who's drunk wine for any length of time. One day, you decide to push the boat out, and the boat sinks. Or perhaps it doesn't sink, it just flounders. Some regions are more prone to floundering wines than others. Burgundy's flounder rate is high, particularly with reds. Ditto for Napa Valley: there are some incredibly ordinary $100 Cabernets out there. And before you fork out big bucks for a wine that's been recommended by a famous critic, make sure you enjoy the cheaper fare that they've also plugged. To reiterate, not everyone likes the same wines.

There is nothing wrong with White Zinfandel...

Given those hundreds of wines on the shelves, surely there's going to be a few that are right up your street... However, go into some snooty wine shops and say you're looking for something similar to your regular Pinot Grigio, and you might as well have trumped in front of the Queen. Once their tsunami of disdain has swept past, they'll say things like, "Well I suppose you could call it wine, but it's not very good, is it?"

And in the general scheme of things, they may have a point. If the finest wine in the world is worth 100 points, then bog-standard Pinot Grigio is probably somewhere in the low teens. But what these snobs can't seem to understand is that for MOST people, wine isn't all that important. If it doesn't taste like paint stripper and the price is right, then they'll buy it. "But surely they must want to trade up to something better?" Er, no. Live with it.

I'll come clean. I'm not a big fan of basic Moscato, Pinot Grigio and White Zin. But I'll always stand up for them for the way in which they get people into drinking wine in the first place. Of these newbies, there'll always be a small proportion, maybe 10% of them, who say, "OK, what's next?" The more people try Pinot Grigio & Co, the greater the number of people who'll want to expand their horizons. Which leads very nicely onto the next section...

The wine that makes you realise that you think about wine more than some other people

To White Zinfandel and Pinot Grigio, I'm going to add Liebfraumilch. It's not the household name it once was, but it used to be guzzled in vast quantities, doing Germany's reputation no good at all in the process.

In my computer system designing days, it was Lieb that lubricated one of the office Christmas lunches. "This is alright," said one of my colleagues. And it was just that – 'alright.' Wet, insipid, alcoholic – and we all probably know people like that. Can't remember what I said in reply, but I do know that two months later, I'd quit the job and was on a plane to Australia.

Taste as much as possible Part 1

Have you ever heard a half-second snatch of music and known exactly what the song was? Or maybe if you didn't know what the song was, then you had a fair idea of what the band was? Repeated listening has somehow caused that music to be ingrained in your memory bank, and it only takes a small stimulus to dig it out again.

It's the same with wine. Someone gives me a glass of wine, and asks me what I think about it. A quick swirl, a quick sniff and...I open my mouth and start talking. And they're amazed. "How can you tell that just from smelling it?"

So I sing to them, "It's fun to stay at the..." And they chip in with "Y-M-C-A!" If I'm really unlucky, they'll do the actions too...

The Village People have taken up residence in their memory banks, and wine can do the same. The more you taste, the more you fill that memory bank, and the easier it becomes to recall the stuff that's in there already. Also, the easier it becomes to get your head around wines you've not tried before – it tastes a bit like this one, mixed with that one, with a little dollop of a third one in there for good measure.

When you first get into music, it's often a case of making blanket judgements such as 'Heavy Metal, Bad; Hip Hop, Good.' And it's the same with wine. Some countries hit the spot, others fall flat. But – back to music – one day you come across a Heavy Metal track you like. Are you going to ignore it as a diversion, or are you going to let your horizons be broadened?

So the bottom line with wine is taste, taste, taste. There'll always be some styles you prefer, but the more you listen to what a wide variety of wines are saying to you, the more you'll enjoy yourself.

The great wine you have to share with too many people
Important and enjoyable as tasting is, wine is meant to be drunk and shared, not sipped and spat. Or sipped once and then rushed on from in been-there-done-that fashion. Went to a wine dinner once where each of the two dozen or more guests had brought at least one special bottle.

We tried 33 wines, all of them top drawer stuff. BUT – and forgive me if this brings to mind gift horses and mouths – we never had a chance to really savour any of them. We moved rapidly though the wine in thimblefuls. We drank too many great wines, but not enough of each one, and in too short a time. That's not what wine is all about...

Taste as much as possible Part 2

Having finished the previous section with an exhortation to taste, taste, taste, you need to know where to start. Two suggestions.

1) Side by side. "It tastes of wine." I've conducted dozens of tastings for the general public, and I regularly hear that line – sometimes uttered under the breath. And the people saying it are absolutely right, it DOES taste of wine.

Which is why I always try to have them tasting at least two different wines at any time, so they can compare and contrast. So yes, they both taste of wine, but is one smoother than the other? Is one sharper, chewier, fruitier than the other? Does one have more of the smoky, toasty imprint of oak? Are they similar in colour?

You can do a similar exercise at home. Buy a couple of bottles of wine and open them on a Friday night. Pour out a glass of each, then screw the cap back on/stick the cork back in and put the bottles in the fridge (yes, including the reds – more about that on p.52). Now try the wines you've poured out. What is it that makes you prefer one to the other? Does that alter when you have them with some food? Does what you can taste agree with any comments on the backs of the bottles?

The next day, pour out another glass of each of the wines and repeat the exercise. Any change? Repeat again on Sunday. By this time, you'll be getting to know these wines quite well, so if you're feeling adventurous, get someone to pour them out without you seeing. Can you tell which is which?

2) Phone a friend. Comparing notes with the backs of bottles is OK, but it's much more fun to do it with friends. So take the idea above, get everyone to bring something to make a reasonable comparison – Pinot Noir, whites at £8-10/$15-20, Chilean Sauvignon Blanc etc – and then start tasting. Don't give yourself too much of each, just enough for a couple of decent mouthfuls. Don't be afraid to say what you think something tastes of – we've got some weird aromas hanging around our memories that occasionally crop up in certain wines.

And if you're feeling bold, you could always do the tasting 'blind'. Fasten newspaper round each of the bottles or shove them into large socks (clean ones please) so all you know is that you're drinking Wine A, Wine B or Wine C. As I said earlier, don't be surprised if not everyone likes the same wines. But also, with identities now all concealed, don't be surprised if people find themselves liking things that they thought they didn't. Speaking of which, let's move on...

The right wine, the wrong occasion

The more you taste, the more likely you are to discover a strange phenomenon, namely wines that you really like but don't want to drink. Maybe you've tried a lovely crisp white wine, but you're on roast beef for dinner. Maybe it's baking hot, and that excellent Cabernet Sauvignon is just a bit burly for the situation.

I came across this a while ago in the middle of a Chilean summer. At the end of a dusty day of winery visits, what we craved was Riesling and Sauvignon Blanc. One night our host decided that we should really be drinking hearty Chilean reds. So he bought one and slammed it down on the table. We dutifully tried it but I don't think many of us finished what was in our glasses...

Good wine does not go out of fashion

"I don't like Riesling, it's too sweet."
"I don't like Chardonnay, it's too oaky."

In all cases, it doesn't have to be, and it often isn't. It's like saying...

"I don't like chicken, it's too spicy."
"I don't like cheese, all those blue veins."

...because you've only ever eaten Red Thai Chicken Curry and Stilton. Just as ten chefs will turn out ten different dishes based on the same ingredients, so winemakers can make a variety of different styles from the same grape. So there is sweet Cabernet Sauvignon and there is dry Riesling. There is oaked Sauvignon Blanc and there is unoaked Chardonnay. Just because some parts of the world used to use a certain grape in a certain way doesn't mean they do so any more. Most German Riesling is now dry, for example, and most current Australian Chardonnays have any oak influence very firmly in the background rather than centre stage.

In fact, let's just try and ditch all wine fashions. It's often a grape variety that is seized upon – Shiraz, Pinot Grigio, Malbec – as THE wine to be seen drinking. Moscato is the fave of the moment, even if large parts of the wine establishment look at many of the current crop of wines rather sniffily. Cue widespread overplanting of the favoured grape round the world, often in quite unsuitable places. To be followed a few years later by a glut as said grape falls from favour...

If it's not a particular grape, then maybe it's a country. Australia is in, Australia is out, Argentina is in, Argentina is out and so on. Or perhaps it's a winemaking style – high alcohol, low alcohol, lots of oak, no oak, blended, unblended etc. etc.

Can we just grow up and ditch the herd mentality? Tarring a whole genre of wines with the same brush – be it a positive or a negative brush – is a mistake. The old Levi's strapline 'Quality Never Goes Out Of Style' applies just as much to wine as to jeans.

So do look at Chardonnay again, do look at Riesling again. And with both, maybe try some Red Thai Chicken Curry and Stilton. Although perhaps not at the same time...

The smug wine
I owe this expression to a lovely lady called Annette Duce who used to head up the wine department at Fortnum & Mason. I'd done her a favour once, so she took me out for lunch at the in-store restaurant. We drank 1970 Vega Sicilia Unico, which many rate as Spain's finest wine. "I call this smug wine," said Annette. "It brings a smile to your face, not just because it's so good, but because you know that no-one else in the room is having anything as good as this." Every once in a while, it's worth treating yourself to a smug wine.

France and Italy: the greatest wines, the grottiest marketing

Let's not beat about the bush, some countries make wine that is dispensable. If Chile or England didn't exist, there wouldn't be too many people in the wine-drinking world who would shed a tear. Unless they came from Chile or England. Ditto for much of Eastern Europe and Canada. But if France or Italy didn't exist...

Sure, both countries produce vast amount of crap wines that no one wants to drink, and sure, other countries make great wine (including Chile & England). But no other places offer such diversity nor such pleasure at all price levels, and nowhere else is the culture of gastronomy so ingrained in the national psyche.

However these attributes, especially the diversity, are also their downfall. You can give a beginner a pretty decent overview of New Zealand wine with about six bottles – and two of those would be Sauvignon Blanc. But many French regions require far more than half a case of wine for you to fully get your head round them, and Italy is if anything even more complicated.

Add in the national character traits – stubbornness for the French, vanity for the Italians – and you have a marketing nightmare. It's no wonder that many people opt for New World wines called simply Blob Estate Cabernet Sauvignon.

But please don't give up on France and Italy. Celebrate and embrace this diversity, look on it not as infuriating but as intriguing. And the best place to begin your exploration is hand in hand with a decent wine merchant – which just so happens to be the subject of the next chapter...

The wine that revives your faith in wine
Linda Davies, you may be a successful novelist, and you may have been taken hostage by a group of Iranian gunboats in 2005. But forever in my mind, you are the person who had a room next to me at college and blighted one of my Sundays by playing Toto's 'Africa' non-stop all afternoon.

It's been a while since I've been so enamoured with a song that I've played it into the ground, but every so often, I come across a wine equivalent, something that stops me in me tracks and makes me marvel at the wonders of fermented grape juice. And it isn't always the expensive stuff that gets the knees trembling and produces the wide smile. A recent example was a 2012 Reuilly from Denis Jamain. On a warm summer day, its combination of crisp fruit and earthy herbal freshness hit the spot beautifully. And of course everyone knows what Reuilly is, and where it comes from. Don't they...?

Find a good, friendly wine merchant

Remember my harsh words for snobby wine merchants a few chapters ago? Those who seem to think we all spend our lives trading up in wine, so that by the time we're 60, we'll be spending a small fortune on our Tuesday night tipple? By the same reasoning, we should all eventually be driving Rolls Royces & living in stately homes...

Thankfully, there are plenty of merchants who have your best interests at heart. Like Julian, for example. Julian manages my local wine shop, and I've watched him in action several times.

His approach isn't rocket science. He finds out the sort of wines people like drinking, or what they're going to be eating that night, and he asks them what they've got to spend. Then nine times out of ten, he picks something that's a pound or two cheaper, and he sends them out of the shop saying, "If you don't like it, just bring it back."

They do come back – and usually not to complain. Then when they've been back a few times and learned to trust him, he starts gently prodding them, challenging them, perhaps suggesting something a little further from their comfort zone, or a little further up the price ladder. Trust first, exploration later. No half-price gimmicks, no vintages of the century, no bullshit, just decent wine and decent service. Simple.

Good wine merchants want to know about you, not just tell you how brilliant their wines are. Find one and your exploration of the wine world (and especially France &

Italy) will be all the more pleasurable. Although do be a little wary if they steer you towards the topic of what's coming next...

The 'I didn't even know that existed' wine

Where once upon a time wine merchants kept much the same stock from year to year, nowadays it can be a case of blink and you'll miss it. Which is why it pays to pop in to see them regularly, even if you don't end up buying something every time.

That's how I found the 1963 Negru de Purkar at the now-defunct Fulham Road Wine Centre. 1963 is my birth year, and it was also a great year for producing port. In most other parts of the wine world however, it was a vintage to forget. But judging by the sip of Negru de Purkar I had in the shop, Moldova (yes, Moldova) seemed to have come up trumps. And it was only £10 a bottle. So I bought a case of the stuff and drank my way through it over the course of the late 1990s.

It was an interesting experience. The corks were about an inch long, and seemed to be kept in place by imitation Elastoplast. As a result, not all of the bottles were great – I think I poured three of them down the sink. But when the wine was good, it was very good, velvety and generous, like warm-hearted old Bordeaux.

Approach natural wine with caution

The UK now has two annual wine fairs where much of the focus is on 'Natural Wines'. The idea of natural wines is that they're made with minimal interference from the producer, with chemical treatments being a no-no in both vineyard and winery. It sounds great in theory, but in practice...

Left to its own devices, wine makes itself. Leave a pile of grapes in a bucket, and the pressure from the ones at the top will crush those on the bottom. Yeast in the air and on the grape skins will set off fermentation of the juice that's oozed out and in no time at all...wine. The first man to discover this probably thought it was amazing, although he'd have had a sore head the morning after. Ditto for second man, and the third, fourth and fifth too.

But it wouldn't have taken long for some bright spark to think of a few tweaks that could improve the process. Crushing the grapes rather than let them do it themselves. Putting a lid on to keep out the flies. Storing the now fully fermented wine in a goatskin to keep it a little fresher.

Step forward thousands of years and thousands of tweaks, and you now have grapes being picked by machines in the middle of the night, computer-controlled crushers, temperature-controlled fermenters and a variety of additives all intended to take the toil out of winemaking. But while the wines emerging from these grape factories may be clean as a whistle, are they really what wine is all about?

No, according to advocates of Natural Wine, it's time to get back to basics and chuck out the jiggery pokery. Let's get musical for a moment. Anyone remember Prog Rock? Twin-necked guitars and ten-minute drum solos? After those indulgent excesses, the late-1970s wave of scruffy spiky weirdos playing two-minute, three-chord ditties came as blessed relief. Natural is the punk rock of wine.

Now while the less-is-more idea is fine in principle, it doesn't mean that making natural wine is easy, or that the wines will be great. Maintaining hygiene is the main problem, and here we'll go from punks to hippies. Take two hippies. One lives on the beach, has a swim every day and sleeps in a hammock, the other lives in a squat in a cold house, and sleeps on an ancient futon. Neither uses deodorant, yet one smells sweet and the other smells...organic.

So it is with natural wines – some are fine, but others reek of stale chicken's innards and cheap cider. And even in the cleaner ones, there often seems to be uniformity of flavour. If the idea is to let the vineyard rather than the winemaking tell the story, why is it often difficult to tell wines from different regions apart?

The French writer and aviator Antoine de Saint Exupéry once said, "A designer knows he has achieved perfection not when there is nothing left to add, but when there is nothing left to take away." With natural wines, many critics feel that the winemakers have gone one little step too far and taken too much away. Rubbish, say their fans, that's how they should be. In our chemically enhanced world, we've forgotten what real wine should taste like.

So who is right? Let's get back to punk rock. Audiences soon tired of bands that had spiky attitude but no talent. However, the good groups persisted and influenced many others. And that's what will (hopefully) happen with natural wines. The bad ones will disappear, the good ones will get even better every vintage, and the philosophy of minimum intervention and reduced use of chemicals will influence other parts of the wine world. Which is surely good for everyone – including punks, hippies and even Genesis fans...

The wine that shows your palate has changed

My daughter's recently discovered my stash of LPs. Golly I bought some shit in my time. Some of it was pressure from friends (Kiss), some because I fancied someone in the band (Altered Images – Claire Grogan, a part of my heart is forever yours), some because I thought I was being trendy (The Pop Group).

But I also bought music that I've simply grown out of. It was right for the time, but that time has passed. And it's the same with wine. I used to be impressed by what I call drum solo wines. I still have a few examples of them gathering dust in my cellar, mostly mid-1990s Australian Shirazes. Now I prefer my wines to whisper – but persistently and seductively...

You should be drinking more fortified wine

Does that need any explanation? Probably. Whenever I do tastings with normal people (as opposed to those like me who spend large amounts of time spitting into a bucket) and there's a fortified wine in the line-up, there's a high likelihood that it will emerge as the most popular wine of the evening. Yet when I ask the audience how often they drink fortified wine, the usual answer is 'hardly ever'. A shame. Let's see if we can do something about that...

A fortified wine is simply one that's had brandy added to it to boost its alcohol content. Sometimes, not much of this spirit is added, and you end up with something not much stronger than a regular table wine. At other times, a major dollop is added, bringing it up to around 20% alcohol – a typical port is a fifth brandy. Some fortifieds are bone dry, others are syruppy sweet, and they come in a wide variety of colours. Wine colours that is – I don't know of any fortified wines that are sky blue...

For those just beginning to get to grips with fortified wines, here are five styles to try, ranging from driest to sweetest:-

Fino Sherry/Manzanilla. Drink it as young as you can find it, well chilled and in proper wine glasses. And once you've opened the bottle, get through it within the next 48 hours. It should be bracingly fresh, like crisp Sauvignon infused with sea air. Great on its own, even better with savoury food – good tapas if you can find it, Kettle Chips if you can't.

Verdelho Madeira. Madeira comes in a variety of sweetnesses: this is towards the drier end of the scale. It combines rich fruit cake flavours with a tangy bite, and as with the fino, is great both by itself and with savoury nibbles. Pretty good with rich fish soups too...

Tawny Port. This is port that's had a fair bit of ageing in barrel, turning from ruby red to, er, tawny in colour. In the process, it also loses both its tannin and fresh fruit flavours, but acquires softer, more mellow dried fruit characters. The most versatile of all ports, you can chill it for summer sipping, serve it with puddings, or bring it out with the Stilton and other semi-hard to hard cheeses.

Banyuls/Maury. Sweeter and maybe not as grown-up as the best port, but these Grenache-based wines from Roussillon in southern France pack a very friendly and potent punch, and are great with dark chocolate mousse.

Rutherglen Muscat. Several countries make good fortified Muscat, but this version from the state of Victoria in Australia is arguably the best. Younger styles are like liquid marmalade tinged with barley sugar, while the venerable, treacly, long-aged wines are like liquid Christmas pudding in a glass.

The best wine ever

'What's your favourite wine?' Wine people get asked this question regularly, and I'm always suspicious of anyone who knows PRECISELY what tops their list. It's like asking what's someone's favourite track, or item of clothing, or place to visit – the answer depends on mood, weather, company and much more besides.

But I can tell you the wine I've given my highest ever score to, back in the days when I used the 100-point scale. Moscatel de Setúbal isn't Portugal's most famous fortified wine, but a tasting of older examples from José Maria da Fonseca revealed that it deserved to be mentioned in the same breath as port and Madeira.

The 20-year-old was delicious, definitely deserving 92 points. Then came a 40-year old wine. It was better. Then we started on the vintage-dated wines. They were better still, and I'd soon reached 100. Heck, I thought, why stop here? My favourite wine was the extraordinary 1900: I gave it 120 points. We finished on the 1880, which was a bit of a come-down, so it only received 110. And that's why I now give wines medals rather than marks...

Food v. non-food wine

Writing the last bit had me salivating, so this might be time to start talking about food and wine. Apparently they can tell the Brits in many European countries because we're the ones who drink wine without food. Of course there's no rule on the backs of bottles forbidding this, but you have to ask why the countries where wine has been drunk for centuries look askance at those who treat wine as a casual everyday drink – who's right and who's wrong?

In truth, you could argue it both ways. Traditionally, wines have been harder and sharper than they are today. Food tempered the acidity (the sharpness) and – in reds – softened the raw tannins (the hardness), allowing the flavours to shine through. Wines from the historic wine producing regions didn't taste actively bad on their own, but they tasted much better with a meal.

Skip to today, and in general wines are far more user-friendly. Lower in acidity, higher in alcohol and far less green and mean in the tannin department, they do taste pretty good by themselves, so why confine them to mealtimes?

Some of today's most expensive and complex wines are of such monumental proportions that they overwhelm virtually all foods – producers of these heady cocktails sometimes suggest that it's best to share a bottle between several people before or after a meal. At the opposite end of the market, if there's a common thread between the cheaper wines in non-trad wine-drinking countries such as the UK, USA and Australia, it's that they're drunk just as much without food – in bars, as a wind-down after a day at work, in front of the TV – as with it.

But there are still plenty of wines that, while tasting reasonable on their own, seem to gain an extra dimension in the presence of food. Chablis is good by itself – but for me it's better with oysters. Rioja gets a new lease of life alongside a plate of roast lamb. Earthy Pinot Noir seems to get richer and earthier with mushroomy dishes.

Does that mean that the wine was inferior in the first place, because it needed some nosh in order to shine? No. Think of them as a partnership – Laurel & Hardy, Starsky & Hutch, Tom & Jerry, something greater than the sum of the parts. What's more, there's something wholesome about sharing wine with family and friends round a table. It loosens the tongue, stimulates the salivary glands and puts a smile on your face.

So I guess I'm siding with the traditional European view on food & wine. But if that's the case, why is there a glass of Sauvignon next to me as I type?

The 'right place at the right time' wine
Following on from the Muscat in the previous chapter, now might be the time to mention the oldest wine I've

ever had. It was in South Africa in 2001. Straight off the plane, I was whisked down to Constantia for lunch. Today Constantia produces a range of excellent red and white wines, but historically, it was famous for the eponymous sweet wine made from the Muscat grape – Jane Austen, Charles Dickens and Baudelaire all refer to it in their writings.

Back to that day in 2001, when one of the local vineyard owners was celebrating his 70th birthday. His son had managed to track down two ancient bottles of Constantia at auction, and they'd just opened one of them. "There's not much left, would you like to try it?" Of course I would. It was the dregs of the bottle, so it was a bit murky, but the wine was still very much alive. It was like high-class marmalade in liquid form, with the syruppy sweetness balanced by tangy citrus acidity. The vintage? 1791.

Food & wine mismatching

Just coming back to a combination like Chablis & oysters, does everyone think they go well together, or is that just me? And remember what I said earlier about not everyone liking the same wines?

I have a tough life. I taste thousands of wines each year, and sometimes — often, in fact — I'm forced to try a few of them over the course of a meal. As I said, tough. But this arduous lifestyle does at least qualify me to talk on the science of food and wine matching. So here, dear reader, are my ten rules on the subject...

- It's bollocks.
- No honestly, it is testicles. The idea — expounded on the back of many bottles — that this wine would be 'The Perfect Match' for such-and-such a dish is just not true. It might be a good match, but 'perfect' implies that serving it with anything less would be close to heresy. I've sat through several meals where several courses were served with several wines to try and determine a perfect match. Was there ever an occasion where everyone agreed on which went best together? No. End of story.

OK, maybe not quite end of story, perhaps there are a few things I've discovered from all that eating and drinking...

- Very very few combinations of food and wine are truly foul. If you find something that is dreadful, have a mouthful of bread and a sip of water and move on.
- Who wears the trousers? Want your food to shine?

Pick a quiet wine. Want your wine to shine? Pick some quiet food. What you don't want is two prima donnas/alpha males fighting for supremacy. 'Quiet' doesn't necessarily mean bland – we're looking for the food/wine equivalent of Richards to Jagger, Sam to Frodo, Wozniak to Jobs, Marr to Morrissey, Wise to Morecambe etc.

- Protein fix. Some wines are acidic, others are tannic, and can be far too chewy by themselves. But have them with strongly flavoured, protein-rich savoury food, especially red meat, and they'll be far friendlier.

- Mopping up the fat. Sausages and ketchup, fish & chips with vinegar, lamb chops with lemon juice... Fatty foods like accompaniments with a bite of acidity. If you find yourself with a wine that's just a bit sharp, try it with the sort of foods you'd serve with something piquant on the side. Riesling with fish & chips. Beaujolais or Bairrada with lamb shanks. I'm now dribbling on the keyboard...

- Soothe that spice. Chilli-rich food needs a touch of softness to calm it down. That softness could be a wine that's low in acidity, which usually means it's from a warm climate, or it could mean a wine with a touch of sweetness. So try things like Chilean Carmenère or off-dry French Pinot Gris. Or Californian Zinfandel. Or whatever else you fancy.

- Cheesed off. There's no such thing as a universal cheese wine, but the closest you'll get to it is probably white. And sweet. Sauternes is renowned for its partnership with Roquefort, but it has many other friends on the cheeseboard.
- Sweet for my sweet. Any wine you serve with pudding has to be sweeter than the food, otherwise it's going to taste sour.
- Ignore all of the above.

The wine where the occasion made the wine taste better

One of my wine life lessons is that I'd rather have a so-so wine with a good friend than a great wine with a prat. Which is why my favourite bottle of sparkling wine ever was the Zonin Prosecco my wife & I drank on the first night of our honeymoon, on a balcony overlooking the Grand Canal in Venice. Perfect.

Don't overchill your whites or overheat your reds

This chapter's all about cola and tea. OK, we might get on to wine at some point, but let's start with cola – ever drunk it warm? Not the most pleasant of experiences. It's bland, it's sweet, it's generally yucky. Chill it a little and – well I still think it's pretty foul, but it's not as bad as it is warm, and it's certainly a fair bit fresher. The cooler temperature has done a couple of things. First it's brought a welcome touch of liveliness to the party, second it's muted some of the flavours – cold coke tastes less sweet than warm.

Now let's move on to tea. Ever let your cuppa go cold and then had a slurp? Remember that bitter assault of tannin in your mouth? Not nice. Yet if you'd supped your brew at the right temperature, then you wouldn't have noticed it anywhere near as much.

So what have we learned? Chilling mutes flavour, enhances freshness and makes tannin stand out. Got that? Let's take that over to wine. Whites first. If your wine tastes as bad as cola, then a week in the fridge will make it fresher and will mute the general grottiness – 'serve well chilled' translates as 'tastes foul at normal temperature'.

But if your wine is rather nice, overchilling means you're in danger of blunting some of that niceness, especially in delicate wines.

And what about tannin? Tannin's more of a factor in reds, but if a white wine has been in a barrel, or if the winemaker has given it a very short period of skin contact (behave at the back, please) in order to extract more flavour from the grapeskins, there'll be some tannin in the wine. Overchill such a wine, and it'll be bitter. We don't want that now, do we? So an hour in the fridge, yes; a week, no...

Now reds. Traditional wisdom has been that reds should be served at 'room temperature', with higher alcohol reds needing a degree or two more of heat. But traditional wisdom doesn't hold true today for two reasons. Firstly, central heating. Room temperature is around 6°C/10°F warmer today than 50 years ago. Secondly, riper grapes. Wines are lower in both acidity (=freshness) and gawky tannin than they used to be.

At today's room temperature, many modern reds are just too gloopy to drink. If they've been stored in such a climate, what they often need is a 15-minute sojourn in the fridge. It's enough to freshen up the flavours but not so much that those tannins start getting too angular.

If anything, with both reds and whites, it's better to slightly overchill than underchill. Warm rooms and warm hands will soon have an effect on slightly-too-chilly wine. But serve wines too warm, and there's not a great deal you can do – although I do know a few people whose personalities could probably lower the temperature of wine a degree or two...

The 'whoops but that was your own fault' wine
Over- and underchilling can be rectified, but there are some wine mistakes you can't correct. I've smashed two £100+ bottles in my time, one through my clumsiness, the other through the collapse of a damp packing case. Grrr... But worse still are those 'mistakes' you make late at night when you've already had enough to drink but feel strangely drawn to open an expensive bottle.

So young wines are guzzled in haste without them having the chance to reveal their true class. Old bottles are roughly handled, resulting in a glassful of murky liquid swimming in cork fragments. Yes, Simon Woods, I'm talking about you and the way you marmalised that 1943 Côte de Beaune that someone had given you as a gift. So stash your really nice wines in a time safe that locks itself at 11pm. And don't wash your nice glasses up until the morning after.

You do not have to finish the bottle

When you cut into a new loaf, do you think, "We're going to have to finish this tonight"? When you've opened a pack of bacon and cooked 2/3 of it, do you say to yourself, "Might as well fry up the rest"? So why do you always feel the need to finish off that bottle of wine in one evening?

Of course, when I say 'you', I don't mean YOU personally, I know you'd never do something like that, but you probably know someone who would. Here's some advice – that you can pass on to that person...

It's true, once you've opened a bottle of wine, it is better to get through it sooner rather than later. It's a rare wine that tastes anything but a shadow of itself a week after it's first opened. But it's also a rare wine that tastes significantly inferior the day after the cork's been pulled or the cap has come off, and if you're careful, you might even stretch this to Days 3 & 4.

You may have seen special pumps to extract air from bottles, or systems involving filling the bottles with inert gas to provide an airtight blanket over your wine. Try them by all means, but you've already got all the wine preservation equipment you need in your kitchen. It's called 'the fridge'.

Next time you open a bottle and don't envisage finishing it, open it and have your glass or two, then put the top back on and bung it in the fridge. Same for white, rosé and red. The less you've had, the longer the bottle will stay fresh. The next day, the red will need a little time to warm up to a reasonable temperature but the whites and pinks should be fine straight from the fridge.

So tell yourself, sorry, your good friends that they don't have to polish off a bottle in a single sitting, and they can even have a number of different wines on the go at any one time.

Or to put it another way...

Fiery Fred could drink no red
His wife could drink no white
So they kept two bottles in the fridge
Which made it all alright

The great wine that lets you down
It should have been a sublime occasion. My parents were visiting us for the first time after the birth of our daughter, and I had a magnum of 1976 Krug to celebrate. I'd tried the wine a couple of years earlier and it had been sublime. Only this time...

You know that period when someone's easing the cork out of a bottle of fizz where everyone else in the room stops talking? Then there's the release – can't remember who said it should sound like a nun breaking wind.

But on this occasion, nature had dealt a hand of no-trumps. The cork stayed put. A little gentle leverage usually does the trick in these situations, but not this time – pliers had to be called for. When the cork eventually came out, the liquid inside the bottle had no fizz, was much deeper in colour than it should have been, and had those tell-tale old-sherry-like notes of oxidation. This was one bottle that we never got round to finishing.

Wine in restaurants: two open letters

Dear Diner,

1) We have tried to select wines we think will go well with the food we offer – please do ask us if you need some advice.
2) If you tell us the sorts of wines you like, we are more likely to be able to recommend something you'll enjoy.
3) Do not say to us, "Is this one any good?" In return, we promise not to say to you, "An excellent choice."
4) If you have chosen a wine and do not like it, please do not tell us the bottle is faulty unless it really is.
5) The reason we have not filled your glass up to the top is…well just have a peak at page 9.
6) If you are having a bad day, please do not take it out on our staff.

Yours,

A Restaurateur

Dear Restaurateur,

1) You offer four starters, four main courses and four desserts – so why confuse us with four hundred different wines?
2) I asked for a recommendation costing £35/$50 – why have you chosen one at £50/$75?
3) I know you have to make money, but you do not need to add the same percentage mark-up to all bottles.

Adding a simple cash mark-up to more expensive wines means I will spend more in your restaurant.

4) If I wanted you to add a thimbleful of wine to my glass every two minutes, I would ask you.

5) Yes, I did just tell you to take that semi-frozen bottle of white out of the ice bucket and replace it with the red, which was at a similar temperature to the soup.

6) When I have ordered a second bottle of the same wine, I still need to taste it – and check it for temperature – before you fill up our glasses.

Yours,

A Diner

The 'can't get enough of it' wine

Normally when wine folk gather for a meal, they want to try a wide variety of wines. But every so often, you get an evening such as the one I spent a while ago in the Millswyn restaurant in Melbourne with a group of sommeliers (and some terrific suckling pig). After trying a Riesling and a Pinot Noir, the third bottle we sampled was the 2009 Oakridge 864 Chardonnay from the Yarra Valley. The fourth bottle was the same, so too the fifth. It was just brilliant, brilliant wine. We smiled a lot that night.

It is worth starting a wine stash

Being a natural product, wine changes with time. Sometimes, this is for the worse – it's a rare Sauvignon Blanc that tastes better at ten years old than at ten months old. But sometimes, it is for the better. Which is why people buy wine to 'lay down' – keep, in other words.

If you're lucky enough to have a house with a cellar, the money to stock it and the willpower to keep your mitts off all those bottles, then great. But even if you're not, there are probably a few nooks and crannies around the house that could be pressed into service – drawers under beds, cupboards under the stairs, space in the bottom of wardrobes and so on.

You're looking for somewhere on the cool and dark side where there's not too much coming and going and where temperatures don't fluctuate greatly. So not the kitchen, and be careful with garages and sheds, which can roast in summer and freeze in winter. If there's no space for a wine rack, you can store the bottles in wine boxes, suitcases, whatever comes to hand. And for a little insulation, smother them in bubble wrap.

How can you tell what's worth keeping? Well, ever had that experience of the last glass of the wine from the bottle tasting significantly better than the first? And not just because you've drunk it all yourself? That wine's a candidate for keeping. Maybe you could try what I suggested in the previous chapter and – with help from the fridge – drink a bottle over the course of a few days. If that wine tasted better on Day 3 than on Day 1, again there's something you can add to your wine stash.

The really cheap stuff's not worth keeping, but here are a few pointers towards some wines that you should be able to buy for ~£10/$15 and which should be all the better for a couple of years' keeping from when they're first released:

Côtes du Rhône Villages
Chianti Classico
Chilean Cabernet
Australian Shiraz
Argentine Malbec
Most Riesling

Why not more whites? Some of them, especially sweet ones, can age brilliantly, but if you have less than perfect storage conditions, reds tend to be more forgiving. As for how long wines can be kept, you're going to have to experiment. With wine as with other things, some people like it young & fruity, others prefer wisdom & experience...

The 'light going on' wine
It was while muddling my way through a degree in Engineering that I had my first 'A-ha!' wine moment. I was supervised for my final year project by an earnest pointy-bearded postgrad called William, a member of the university wine society.

I usually ignored the recommendations he passed on to me, but one day he got particularly hot under the collar about a Rioja, namely the Viña Real Gran Reserva 1973. So I bought a bottle. Oo La La. How could fermented grape juice be transformed into something so mellow yet refreshing, so intense in flavour yet light in body, so svelte and sexy? I was hooked. And still am.

And to finish...

...And hopefully you've gained a little bit of wisdom over the course of the last 21 chapters, and you'll be getting to work on the experience as soon as possible. We've only scratched the surface of the surface of wine in this book, but hopefully there's enough food (and wine) for thought for the moment.

If you've enjoyed the book, I'd love to hear your comments – send an email to shortest@simonwoods.com, or contact me through Twitter, where I'm @woodswine. I'd be particularly keen to hear what you'd like to learn next about wine, then I can address that in a future book.

And remember, there are three extra chapters up for grabs – just go to simonwoods.com/shortest-chapters, fill in the box there, and that will also put you on the list to receive my weekly newsletter.

Is that glass you started the book with empty now? Maybe time to go for a refill.

Simon Woods
November 2013, revised July 2014

Fancy more of Simon's thoughts on wine? Then why not sign up for his weekly newsletter? "What wonderful things they are," said one subscriber. Posted every Tuesday, around lunchtime-ish (UK time), they're intended to make you think and smile, hopefully in equal measure. You can sign up at simonwoods.com.

And keep an eye out for a new edition of Simon's book 'I Don't Know Much About Wine But I Know What I Like.' The first edition was the Champagne Lanson Wine Book of The Year in 2003, and this new edition has been fully updated and is scheduled to go on sale in autumn 2014.

Finally, Simon is a popular and entertaining speaker on a wide variety of wines and wine regions. If you'd like to work with him, get in touch through simonwoods.com.

About the author

Wine Consultant, Author and Speaker Simon Woods has won awards for his writing, his website and his can-can dancing. While he spits out most of the many thousands of wines he tastes each year, he does confess to swallowing a few of them.

When he's not visiting vineyards, tasting with importers and retailers, or hosting one of the dozens of wine events he conducts each year, he can be found at home in Saddleworth in the north of England with his wife & two children.

Website:	www.simonwoods.com
Twitter:	@woodswine
Facebook:	facebook.com/simonwoodswine